CH00956327

SHIRE NATURAL HIS

ANTS
of the British Isles

GARY J. SKINNER

CONTENTS

COVER: *Red ant workers (Myrmica sp) tending aphids on a thistle. These ants tend aphids less commonly than many other species.*

Series editors: Jim Flegg and Chris Humphries.

Set in 9 point Times roman and printed in Great Britain by C. I. Thomas & Sons (Haverfordwest) Ltd, Press Buildings, Merlins Bridge, Haverfordwest, Dyfed.

Introduction

Ants are one of the best known groups of insects, encountered frequently in the house, in the garden and, often annoyingly, on a picnic. There are very few people who would not be able to recognise ants. They are quite unusual insects in being generally wingless, although certain members of a colony are winged. There are some insects which look superficially like ants and are also without wings. The best known of these are the velvet ants, whose large size (½ inch, 13 mm), striking markings (orangy thorax, silver hairs on the abdomen) and straight antennae immediately distinguish them from any British ant. These insects are quite rare. There are also some small wingless wasps which might be confused, at first sight, with ants, but the shape of the antenna, which is straight in all these, distinguishes them from the ants, in which the antenna is elbowed. Furthermore, in all ants, bees and wasps there is a waist, but in the ants this is scale-like or has projections, or nodes, on it.

Perhaps the characteristic by which ants are most usually identified is their numbers. Being generally social insects, they are normally seen in large numbers and this immediately identifies them as ants. No other British insects combine the two features of winglessness and social organisation although in other parts of the world, including southern Europe, termites (sometimes called white ants) show these two features.

The ants all belong to one family, the Formicidae, within the insect order Hymenoptera. This order contains bees and wasps as well as the ants. There are over ten thousand species of ant in the world, belonging to eleven subfamilies. In Britain there are a mere fifty or so species, in four subfamilies. The largest British subfamily is the Myrmicinae, which consists of all the ants with a two-segmented waist. Next come the Formicinae, which have only one segment in the waist. The last two British subfamilies also have one segment to the waist but each has only one species. They are the Dolichoderinae, represented by Tapinoma erraticum, and the Ponerinae, represented by the rare Ponera coarcta.

Of the British ant species, only a few are at all common and likely to be encountered by the amateur naturalist. The following can be taken as a general set of rules for identifying the commoner species (see also the Simple identification guide at the end of the book). Small black ants are almost certainly Lasius niger, and small yellow ones are Lasius flavus. Any large ant (0.3 inch, 8 to 10 mm) encountered is likely to be a wood ant (Formica) or a member of the non-wood ant section of the genus Formica. If it is reddish brown it is a wood ant; if it is dull black it is a non-wood ant (probably lemani or fusca). In southern Britain

1. *A diagram of a worker of the wood ant Formica rufa. This ant is typical of the family Formicinae, with a single-segmented waist. The diagram shows the main parts needed for identification.*

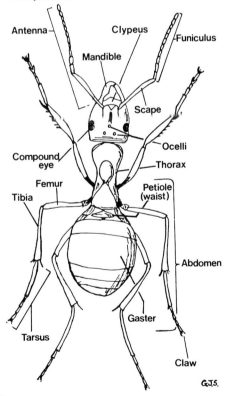

2

2. Worker of an ant in the genus Myrmica. This ant is typical of those in the family Myrmicinae with a two-segmented waist. All features unlabelled have the same names as those in figure 1.

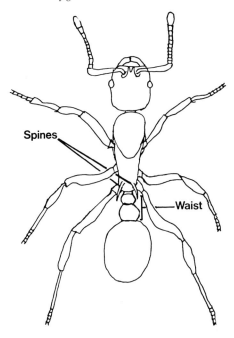

wood ants encountered will almost certainly be *Formica rufa*. In the north of England and in Scotland the very similar *F. aquilonia* and *lugubris* will be seen. Very careful examination of many workers is needed to separate these three species. Very rarely the Slave-making Ant *(Formica sanguinea)*, which is very like a wood ant, may be found but it occurs only in a few localities in the south and in the Cairngorm region of Scotland. The only other quite large species is *Lasius fuliginosus* and this can be immediately told from any other ant by its very shiny black colour and the deep notch at the back of the head.

Medium-sized red ants with two segments in the waist will almost certainly be of the genus *Myrmica*. There are eight British species and it is an expert job to separate them. Some of the books listed on page 24 will help in this, particularly that by M. V. Brian.

The only problems likely to be encountered with these simple rules are as follows:

1. Large ants may be the sexuals (reproductive caste) of species with small workers. These will be easily distinguished because they will be seen winged or, if they have lost their wings, because of the more robust nature of the thorax.

2. The ant *Leptothorax acervorum* is common in Britain and is very *Myrmica*-like. It is not easily distinguished from the *Myrmicas*, but the last three segments of the antennae are longer than is found in *Myrmica*.

3. *Tetramorium* is a brownish to black ant found on heathland and may be confused with *Lasius niger*, but it has two segments in its waist, while *niger* has only one.

4. *Tapinoma erracticum* is very like *Lasius niger* at first sight but has no body hair, unlike *niger*, which is quite hairy, so it can be fairly easily distinguished with a hand lens.

All other British ants are very local in distribution, mostly being found in the central southern counties of Hampshire and Dorset and in the Channel Islands.

All ants are social and live in colonies with three *castes:* females (the queen or queens), males and workers. There are a few very interesting British species which live as social parasites of different degrees; one has abandoned having workers of its own species and uses those of another species to do all its work. This is the so-called Workerless Ant *(Anergates atratulus)*.

COLONIES

In those ants in which colony structure is fairly normal, the majority of the insects to be found in a nest are *workers*. These are fundamentally females and occasionally lay eggs but they must be regarded as sexually immature. They take no direct part in the reproduction of the colony, even those occasional eggs which they do lay being used as food. These individuals are always without wings. They sometimes show division of labour and of size. In some non-British species there may be workers of vastly different head and body sizes and form. In British species, however, variations are limited to a range from small to large

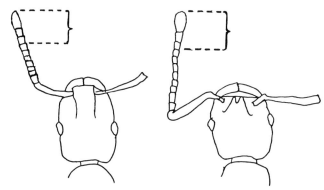

3. *The antennae of the genera Leptothorax (left) and Myrmica (right) compared. In Leptothorax the last three segments are about the same length as all the other small segments together. In Myrmica these three segments are much shorter.*

workers. In wood ants *(Formica rufa),* for example, the smallest workers are a little under 0.2 inch (5 mm) in length and the biggest a shade over 0.4 inch (10 mm). The lack of definitely different worker forms in the British species, however, does not indicate that they do not show division of labour. It has been clearly shown that some workers spend their time collecting honeydew from plant lice (aphids and scale insects), while others may be tending young (brood) and still others will be repairing the nest.

Queen ants without wings may be found in nests at any time of year, the number present varying from species to species, being only one in some cases and many hundreds in others. A single queen is a rarity in British ant species. The queens are generally bigger than the workers, although this is not universally true. In the common species *Lasius niger* and *flavus* queens exceed the workers in size by a considerable margin, being perhaps twice as long. In the wood ants the difference is not so great. Apart from the size differences, workers and queens can be quite easily distinguished on other grounds. The most obvious difference is the size of the thorax. This is the part of the body which carries the wings and the muscles which operate them. Since workers never have wings their thorax is small and tubular. In the queens, on the other hand, the possession of wings in early life necessitates a large thorax to accommodate the muscles. Since the exoskeleton is hard, even though the muscles are lost after the wings have been, the large

thoracic compartment is still visible in queens of any age. The *gaster,* or rear part of the abdomen, of the queen is generally much bigger than that of a worker of the same species because it is here that the ovaries are housed. Workers, as already suggested, may have ovaries but they are much shorter and less branched than the queen's, so the gaster is consequently smaller. In addition to this, the queen's gaster contains a sperm sac, which is never present in that of the worker. It is here that sperm, from her one and only mating, are stored for the rest of her life, ready to fertilise eggs.

At certain times of year winged queens and winged males are produced. The males are distinguishable from the queens on a variety of structural grounds. In all species the gaster of a male has one more segment visible than that of queens or workers. In the two-petioled ants the male has six gaster segments and the queen five, and in one-petioled species the male has five gaster segments while the queen has four. In addition the male genitalia are usually fairly obvious at the end of the abdomen. In some species the sex difference is more obvious even than this with the males being much smaller than their potential mates. This is the case in the common garden species *Lasius flavus* and *L. niger.*

The role of these so-called *sexuals* is to fly, mate and then, in the case of the queens, to attempt to found new nests away from the parent. This ensures dispersal of the species across the available suitable environment and it also avoids

4

10 (above left). *Workers of Lasius flavus in the soil of their mound.*

11 (above right). *Workers and winged queens of Lasius fuliginosus. The insects are shiny black with a deeply notched head.*

12 (below). *A typical rockery or pavement nest of Lasius niger, to be found in most gardens.*

aphids for honeydew. The two species are distinguished by the degree of hairiness of the middle and hind femora, *lemani* being a much hairier ant in this respect than *fusca*, which is virtually hairless in these regions of its legs.

Of the other native British species, few are to be expected in the garden. *Tetramorium caespitium* may sometimes be found in lawns, but it is most typically a heathland or duneland species (see the next chapter). This is another species whose distribution is mainly southern, although it has been found in coastal sand dune sites as far north as the Firth of Forth.

Ants of heathland

Heathlands, both in Scotland and in the south of England, have been intensively studied, mainly by Michael Brian, in relation to the ants living in them. Ants are animals which basically require warm conditions and the often sandy soil of heaths provides these. Typical of such heathland habitats, most particularly in the south, is the Yellow Hill Ant, *Lasius flavus*, already mentioned as a species often found in the garden. On open heath or pasture where disturbance, such as that experienced on a mown lawn, is rare this species can build mound nests of earth. In studies in the south densities as high as 1500 such mounds per hectare (600 per acre) have been reported. The nests are often evenly spaced where they are densest, suggesting that each colony is avoiding the others. They are about a foot (30 cm) or so high and about the same in diameter. The soil that forms the above-ground portion of the nest is sometimes slightly less acid than the surrounding soil and this may account for some of the differences in the vegetation of the mound that have been found. The ability of plants to withstand having soil heaped around them regularly is another factor which is important in determining what lives on the mound.

In this type of habitat the other common species are those of the genus *Myrmica*. Where conditions are wetter, *Lasius flavus* is unable to nest because of the waterlogged nature of the soil. Ants are not absent, however, because dry sites can be found for nest construction and if foraging is mainly above ground, as it is in *Myrmica*, survival is possible. One species, *Formica transkaucasica*, is restricted to this type of bog habitat.

In southern moorland some ants not generally encountered in the garden may be found. *Tetramorium caespitium* is one of the commonest. The colonies are large, with a few thousand individuals being typical. The species is mainly a carnivore and seems to tend aphids only rarely. It shows a very big disparity between the size of the workers and that of the sexuals. The workers are less than 0.2 inch (4 mm) whereas the queens may be as much as 0.4 inch (8 mm). A habit of *T. caespitium* is the collection of seeds, which are stored in the nest. It is thought that these seeds may form a food source in early spring when other materials are scarce.

As in many other habitats, *Lasius niger* is found in southern heaths, but a different *Lasius*, *alienus*, is found there too. This species nests in the soil. *Formica fusca*, discussed as a garden species, is also found in this habitat.

Another small ant to be found in heathland is the only British member of the family Dolichoderinae, the locally distributed *Tapinoma erraticum*. This makes very small 4 inch (10 cm) nests with a covering of debris. The workers are small (0.2 inch, 3 to 4 mm) and very active, constantly running about in warm conditions. It is basically a scavenger and finds bits and pieces of dead insects, often other ants killed in territory squabbles, to eat. Unlike all other British species, *Tapinoma* has no readily visible defences: the Ponerines and Myrmicines have a sting and the Formicines a formic acid gland. *Tapinoma's* quick movements may give some defence and it has also been shown to have a gland which produces offensive liquid.

A number of *Myrmica* are likely to be encountered on heaths, more species in the south. *M. ruginodis*, *scabrinodis* and

13. *Mounds of Lasius flavus. These mounds often occur at very high density in fields and alter the pattern of vegetation on their surfaces.*

sabuleti are the commonest.

Formica transkaucasica has already been mentioned and another *Formica, cunicularia,* also occurs on heaths. This is quite a rare ant. It looks rather like a brown, hairy *fusca* and sometimes builds a mound nest. Specimens should be carefully checked against a good key because *fusca* also occurs in this habitat.

Because of the presence of *Tetramorium*, its two parasites, *Anergates atratulus* and *Strongylognathus testaceus,* are also found. These species are both uncommon and very difficult to find. *Anergates* is the more highly developed as a parasite. The species has no workers and the males are very degenerate, being wingless and pupoid in form. They are fed by *Tetramorium* workers and seem to be incapable of eating without such assistance. The males and females mate in the host nest but the queens then fly away to seek new hosts. The effect on the host is that nests of *Tetramorium* infested by *Anergates* do not have queens, males or larvae. This means that the *Tetramorium* nest will die out and so, therefore, will the *Anergates*.

The other social parasite of *Tetramorium*, *Strongylognathus*, has workers of about the same size as the hosts, but its queens are much smaller and contrast with the relatively large host queens. The workers' mandibles are very simple and they are not known to forage for food, being fed by host workers. The host queen does not produce sexuals when parasitised, but she does continue to produce workers. The *Strongylognathus*, on the other hand, produce many sexuals and must be considered as a successful parasite.

Ants of woodlands

Because ants like sunny positions woodlands would seem to be an unpromising habitat in which to find them, but woods are an excellent place to study ants because they contain nests of the most striking of British species, in terms of the size of both individuals and colonies. These are the ants of the so-called *Formica rufa* group, the red wood ants. These ants are the only truly woodland species in Britain. Their ability to conserve heat within the nest and to walk the long distances from nests to tree tops allows

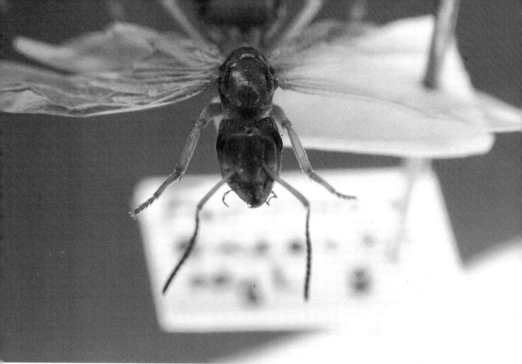

14. *Head of Formica exsecta, from above, the head facing down the page. Note the deep notch at the back of the head which easily distinguishes this from other species in this genus.*

15. *Wood ants (Formica aquilonia) dragging a scaly weevil back to the nest. Such food is brought back mainly to feed brood.*

16. *Wood ants (Formica rufa) tending aphids on the leaf petioles of sycamore.*

17. *Lasius niger tending aphids on a foxglove. The ant on the right is just taking a droplet.*

them to colonise this generally unsuitable environment.

In Britain there are six species of the *Formica rufa* group, only three of which are likely to be encountered by the amateur naturalist. In the south of England and Wales, as far north as north Lancashire in the west but only to Lincoln in the east, is to be found *F. rufa* itself. Further north in England and in Scotland is found *F. lugubris*. Found in Scotland only, and spreading as far north as Wester Ross, is *F. aquilonia*.

18. *Drawings of the heads of British Formica (except pratensis). Only those features important in identification have been added in each diagram. (A) F. rufa. No obvious hairs on the top or sides of the head or on the eyes. (There may be the occasional short hair here.) (B) F. aquilonia. Some hairs on top of the head but not very many down the sides and sometimes absent. Eyes with some hairs. (C) F. lugubris. The sides and top of the head usually with many long hairs. This often gives rise to a fringe below the eyes. Eyes hairy. (D) F. exsecta. Told from all others by the deeply notched (excised) head. (E) F. sanguinea. Told from all others by notched clypeus (arrowed).*

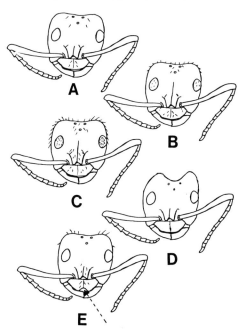

A

B

C

D

E

To the casual observer these species are all very similar. Some of the differences between them, and two of the other species, are shown in figure 18. Two of the other red *Formicas, Formica exsecta* and *F. pratensis*, are so rare that they are infrequently met, although *F. exsecta* is strikingly different from the others, having a deeply excised back to its head, so it should be easily identified if it is found. Its distribution is strange in that it occurs in the area around Bournemouth in the south, in the Spey valley district of the highlands of Scotland and nowhere else. *F. pratensis* is very local in south Hampshire but is common in the Channel Islands, where it is the commonest species. It is very similar to the other *rufa* group ants but tends to build very different nests, often from sand. The sixth red *Formica* ant is not strictly a wood ant and is mentioned later.

Wood ant workers are up to 0.4 inch (10 mm) or slightly more in length and thus these are by far the biggest of the British species. Colonies are similarly large, with up to half a million individuals being found in a single nest. The nests, except those of *Formica pratensis*, are made partially of twigs or, in pine woods, needles. The dome, however, is only the above-ground portion of the nest and the structure extends at least as deep underground with interconnecting galleries. It is thought that the domed portion of the nest is important in catching heat for the ants, which, being cold-blooded, rely on heat for activity.

All the wood ants show a very high degree of social organisation in food hunting as well as other activities. On any day after the end of the winter workers can be seen streaming from the nest along 'roads' kept clear of obstructions by their own actions. Along the same roads workers also stream back and a short period of observation will show that they do so with many and varied loads. This group of species carries a wide range of food back to the nest. Observations have shown that in a single day in summer the workers from a typical *Formica rufa* nest bring back over sixty thousand individual items, including aphids (greenfly), booklice, caterpillars, beetles, flies, harvestmen, woodlice and even pieces of plant

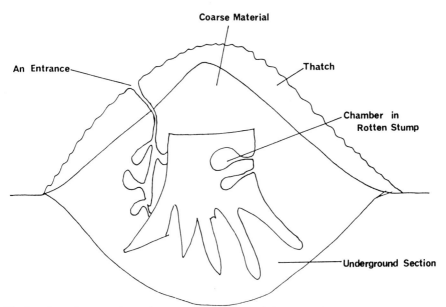

Coarse Material

An Entrance

Thatch

Chamber in Rotten Stump

Underground Section

19. *Drawing of a typical wood ant nest, showing the below-ground structure.*

material. The last would be partially for nest repair and consist of twigs and pine needles, but seeds are brought back for consumption of the special 'oil bodies' that some plants (such as the violets) produce for the ants. The ants serve the function of dispersing the seeds.

A very important source of food for all wood ants is aphid (greenfly) honeydew. Aphids feed on the sugary sap inside plants and derive all the sugar and protein they need from it. Because the sap contains very little protein but a relatively large amount of sugar, the aphids have to consume far more sugar than they need in order to get enough protein. They consequently excrete a lot of sugar solution, which is called honeydew. That ants relish sugar can be confirmed by putting out sugar bait for them and, indeed, it is well known that they will flock to sugary cakes and jams. The ants find the excretions of the aphids irresistible and tend them, rather in the way that man tends cows for milk. Indeed, aphids are often referred to as 'ant cows'.

This relationship between ant and aphid is an example of a symbiosis in which both partners benefit and is called a mutualism. The ants get food and the

aphids are protected from their enemies, such as ladybirds and lacewing flies, which the ants eat. They are also cleaned by the ants and their rate of reproduction is speeded.

Many aphid species rely entirely on ants. They are structured in a number of ways that encourage milking. In the non-tended aphids there are two structures on the abdomen called cornicles. These produce a sticky wax and serve to deter many natural enemies. Tended species do not have these cornicles or they are small and non-functional. In addition, the tended species hold their honeydew on the end of the abdomen so that the ants can easily lick it; in the non-tended species the droplet is flicked away from the animal very forcefully.

These ants are usually violent predators, so why do they not kill the aphids but tend them instead? It appears that the resemblance between the posterior of an aphid and the front of an ant, together with the offer of sugar, is enough to suppress predatory tendencies. A few minutes' observation of wood ants will show that they are willing to attack almost everything else.

At the height of the season in late May

15

20. *A wood ant in a typical aggressive posture, squirting formic acid at the photographer.*

21. *The Slave-making Ant, Formica sanguinea, with a slave pupa.*

22. *The myrmecophilous woodlouse Platyarthrus hofmannseggii in the nest of Lasius niger. It is found commonly in such nests in gardens.*

23. *Larva of the Large Blue, Maculinea arion, about to be adopted by a Myrmica sabuleti worker.*

the ants bring about 50 mg of sugar to the nest every five minutes. This amount is about half a pound (0.25 kg) of sugar a day, and the seasonal total, allowing for adjustments in the rate of collection, is about 100 pounds (46 kg). In terms of wet weight of sugar solution carried back, this is about 600 pounds (275 kg) or over a quarter of a ton of solution carried to a single nest in one season!

The other food eaten is needed mainly for the development of the young (brood). As we have seen, honeydew contains little protein, insufficient for the growth and development of young, so the honeydew diet is supplemented by protein-rich insect carcasses. At the height of the season wood ants bring back as much as 5 ounces (about 140 grams) of solid food in a single day, amounting to 10 pounds (about 5 kg) of solid food in the month of May. Such large rates of food consumption may be expected to have some effect on the populations of animals which are eaten (see the chapter on 'Ants and Their Environment').

Apart from taking food from the wood, ants also act as food for other woodland animals. One of the best known is the Green Woodpecker *(Picus viridis)*, which eats hibernating ants in large numbers in winter. One study has shown that the number eaten may be as high as fifteen per cent of the total population of the nest, which would be about 75,000 ants. Other animals which eat wood ants are badgers and a range of small specialised beetles, which are dealt with later.

Wood ants have the same basic reproductive biology as all other ant species as described earlier. The winged males and females of the *Formica rufa* group fly in May and mate in tree tops and on the wing. The method of nest establishment by a mated queen may, however, be different from the usual pattern. After the flight the queen sheds her wings and then finds a nest of another *Formica* ant (not a member of the wood ant group but *Formica fusca*). When she has found a small colony she enters it and collects a few *fusca* pupae around herself. She may build a small cell for defence. When the *fusca* pupae emerge the workers associate with the *rufa* queen and kill the original *fusca* queen. The eggs of the *rufa* queen are looked after by the *fusca* workers until they hatch into adult workers. These then take over the nest, which rapidly becomes *rufa* only. This way of establishing a nest is called temporary social parasitism.

Wood ants have a remarkably well developed ability, as a colony, to maintain and defend their own territory. The conditions inside the nest, where brood develops, are much less variable than those in the environment outside. Enormous care is lavished by the ants on their nest building. As much as half of all loads brought to the nest may be plant material for nest repair.

This elaborate nest is important to the ants for temperature regulation and to protect them from rain. Temperatures on the surface of mounds may vary as much as 15 degrees Celsius (27 degrees Fahrenheit) in summer but deep inside the nest variation is only a degree or so, being kept at an even 25 C (77 F). Thrusting one's hand into a nest will show this: the feeling is rather like that one might imagine in a very slow oven. Just below mound surfaces temperatures are quite a lot higher than this and it is here that pupae (often called 'ant eggs' and used as fish food) are to be found. They are being 'forced' to develop more quickly.

The smooth surface of the nest is maintained by the constant activity of the workers and is important for the shedding of rainfall.

The workers defend the nest vigorously against all comers and are well equipped to do so. Like all ants they have relatively powerful jaws and they are armed with a large stock of poisonous formic methanoic acid, which is believed also to act as an alarm signal to other workers. Up to 45 per cent of a wood ant's weight is formic acid. Stirring a group of workers on the nest surface will cause the expulsion of large quantities of this acid, giving rise to a powerful smell. Most people would not want to thrust their arms into nests of wood ants and it would not be good for the ants, but it was once believed to be a very effective relief for rheumatism.

Careful stirring of just a small part of

18

the nest surface can be used to demonstrate the 'signal' function of the acid. The disturbance caused by the stirring can be seen to spread rapidly to most of the nest surface. This little experiment is most effective in spring when large workers gather on the nest surface in what are known as 'spring masses'. The function of this massing in early spring is not clearly understood, but a suggestion is that the ants are carrying heat into the nest to enable it to resume functioning after the winter sleep.

The ants are well equipped to deliver the poisonous load of acid. They can bite with their powerful jaws and then squirt acid into the wound from the abdomen, causing death to small insects and a little pain to a human being. The abdomen is very flexible and allows the ant to squirt acid in a forward direction.

Outside the nest, the workers are just as vigorous in the defence of their territory, which may extend over 100 yards (90 metres) in all directions, although the shape of the territory is determined by the presence of other competing nests. Indeed, competitors in the form of other *Formica* colonies are probably the biggest enemies of a particular nest. It is not surprising, then, that wood ants expend a lot of energy in defending their territories from others. The ants are able to recognise members of their own colony, probably due to the presence of a 'nest odour', and viciously attack strangers.

The most striking demonstration of this aggression to strangers is during the so-called 'spring battle'. In the early part of the year, after hibernation, territory boundaries are re-established and this often leads to a major battle between the ants of one nest and those of an adjacent one. In a typical battle large numbers of workers are to be found at a point between the two combatant nests. Workers are locked in fierce fighting, the smell of formic acid is overpowering for a number of feet around the battle ground, and dead workers are being carried back in streams to both nests.

In one of the British species, *Formica lugubris,* which is found in the north of England and some parts of Scotland, this aggressive behaviour is not quite so marked and there are communications between nests, a wood often being full of nests of many sizes ranging from mature to very young. These are interconnected and, probably, there is some reproduction by budding of nests. This means that in this species the mated queen appears to re-enter her own nest and form a new one with a band of workers from the old parent nest. Indeed, the different pattern of nest distribution is a good way of helping to recognise the presence of this species in the field.

Now rare in Britain, *Formica sanguinea* is very like *rufa* in appearance. However, its nests are quite different, being simple thatched soil mounds, and its habits are very different too, for this is the so-called Blood-red Slave-making Ant.

The pattern of a *Formica sanguinea* raid is quite complex but, essentially, the workers surround the nest of the species to be raided, often *F. fusca*. The *F. fusca* very often flee, leaving their pupae. These the *F. sanguinea* take back to their nest. Some are eaten, but the rest are reared and emerge as workers, which then look after the *sanguinea* brood, as slaves.

Apart from the *Formica* species there are a few other ants whose main habitat can be thought of as woodland.

Living in the nests of wood ants can occasionally be found the rare guest species *Formicoxenus nitidulus*. Unlike *Anergates,* previously mentioned, *Formicoxenus* has a worker caste and a whole colony within a colony exists. It is found only with *Formica rufa*, where it seems to avoid attack by its greater speed, although the wood ants seem generally to ignore it. It appears that the host workers feed the guests.

Another ant which can be most conveniently regarded as a woodland species is the very rare *Stenamma westwoodi*. This species is small in all respects. Its workers are only up to 0.2 inch (3 to 4 mm) long and colonies have generally less than one hundred individual workers. The food of the ant seems to be mainly insect flesh. The most characteristic feature is the minute eyes of the workers, which immediately distinguish it from any other species.

A common species frequently found in

24. *A nest of the wood ant Formica aquilonia in a Scots pine forest. The trowel is 10 inches (25 cm) long.*

woodland, but not restricted to it, is *Leptothorax acervorum* (see Introduction). Small in size, it forms colonies of less than a hundred individuals. In woodland these are often in very hard wood in tree stumps or even inside twigs and it may therefore easily be overlooked.

There are three other *Leptothorax* recorded in Britain but all are very rare and found only very locally in the south.

Ant associations

It is not surprising that such highly organised and abundant insects as the ants have associations with many other species of animal. Their use of aphids for food and the eating of ants by woodpeckers have already been mentioned. However, many other associations occur within and around the nest. These are with the so called 'guests' of the ants (myrmecophiles), and despite the basical-

ly aggressive nature of ants hundreds of species have been recorded as guests.

A wide range of insect and other groups are potential guests, including beetles (Coleoptera), various Hymenoptera (small wasps), moth and butterfly larvae (Lepidoptera), flies (Diptera), bugs (Hemiptera), spiders, mites, woodlice, roundworms and even the Slowworm *(Anguis fragilis),* a legless lizard. This chapter describes some of the guests most likely to be found by the amateur naturalist.

Ant guests have various motives for their associations. In some cases the ants themselves seek out the guests, as with aphids, scale insects (Coccidae) and the caterpillars of the blue butterflies (Lycaenidae), and both the ants and the guests benefit from the relationship. In other cases the guest seeks out the ants and the ants may be indifferent to its presence or it may even be harmful to them. The true guests, those the ants bring in, are often fed and licked, while other kinds are ignored and yet others are not tolerated but nevertheless still live with the ants and may eat them or their larvae. Finally, there are the parasites that live on, or in, the ants or their young.

Perhaps the most commonly seen ant guest is the small, white woodlouse *Platyarthrus hofmannseggii*. This species is very often present in nests of *Lasius* and other species in the south, although its range does extend to the north of England. The ants seem to ignore it but it is absolutely dependent on them, feeding on scraps of food in the nest. It is also thought to accompany ants to the branches on which aphids are being milked in order to drink honeydew.

The insect order with the most numerous and varied myrmecophiles is the Coleoptera (the beetles). Beetle guests of all kinds occur. Of the true guests, *Atemeles* is one of the most interesting. There are two British species, *Atemeles emarginatus* and *A. paradoxus*. They produce a secretion which is very attractive to the ants and they are able to mimic the behaviour of workers, so their safety is ensured. They are known also to feed on eggs and larvae in the nest. *Atemeles* are to be found in nests of *Formica fusca* and *Myrmica* species. Other true beetle guests include *Claviger longicornis,* found with *Lasius* species, *Lomechusa strumosa,* which is found only with *F. sanguinea,* and *Amphotis marginata,* which is found with *Lasius fuliginosus.*

Many species of beetles live as lodgers which the ants appear to ignore. Most of these belong to the rove beetle family, Staphylinidae. These are easily recognised by their very short wing cases and elongated shape. The wood ants have many such guests, which can be easily collected by placing a brick or slate on the thatched nest. If this is removed after a few days, many beetles may be found underneath it.

An important genus of Staphylinid beetles is *Myrmedonia*. The Myrmedonias lurk on trails and attack and devour large numbers of workers. The ants may attack them but the beetles have various means of protecting themselves. They produce a powerful vapour which causes ants to break off any attack very quickly. They often escape attack by feigning death and many of them closely resemble their hosts and may therefore be ignored.

The caterpillars of the Lycaenidae, or blue butterflies, are one of the most interesting groups of myrmecophiles. They produce secretions which attract ants and thus they collect workers around themselves. They have a tough outer skin and they do not defend themselves when surrounded by workers. Attracting ants in this way is thought to protect them from predators. In one species, *Maculinea arion* (the Large Blue), which used to occur in Britain but was declared extinct there in 1979, the third instar larva is collected by ants of genus *Myrmica,* which take it into their nest. There it feeds on ant larvae and is fed by the ants with the chewed-up material they feed to their brood, to emerge as an adult butterfly in June. The ants tolerate it because of the secretions it produces, which they cannot resist, even though it is eating their larvae.

Ants have a number of external and internal parasites, but all are small and unlikely to be encountered unless particularly looked for. One of interest is the Lesser Liver Fluke *(Dicrocoelium dendriticum)*. This has a number of stages during its larval life, one being within the ant *Formica fusca.* Eggs of the fluke leave an infested sheep and enter a snail, where they go through a number of stages, eventually to leave in slime balls, which are eaten by the ants. The larvae encyst in the ant's abdomen, re-entering sheep when the animals accidentally eat the ants.

Ants and their environment

Like man, ants are very abundant and show a high degree of social organisation. It might therefore be expected that, like man, they would have a major effect on the environment in which they live. Studies have shown that this is indeed so. They can affect the number of the animals and plants upon which they feed, both positively and negatively. They affect the structure and quality of the soil, which has important implications for the farmer and gardener. Because of these effects ants can be pests to man, but they can be allies too. We may need to control them in some situations, such as when they invade our buildings, but wholesale destruction may not be in man's best interests.

The predatory nature of ants has already been noted. The predation of very large and abundant species, such as the wood ants, may have a significant effect on prey populations. It has been noted on many occasions, in woods suffering a major attack by caterpillars which defoliate trees, that those trees in the vicinity of wood ants' nests are hardly touched. They represent what some German entomologists have referred to as 'green islands' in a sea of destruction. In one study in northern Britain it was shown that in ant-infested areas only one per cent of leaf area was removed from oaks whilst at the same time in a nearby and very similar uninfested area eight per cent of the leaves were being removed by the caterpillars that eat them. Since it is the leaves which make the food which is turned into wood, this would seem to have possible implications for the control of pests of timber-producing trees. The experimental introduction of wood ants into areas where timber trees are grown has been tried with some success. There is, however, one drawback. As we have seen, ants tend aphids for their honeydew secretions and in doing so protect the aphids from their natural enemies. Although aphids do little obvious damage to the trees, their removal of sap and the possibility that they might transmit disease to the trees make them very serious pests. So, although ants may be protecting the tree from caterpillars, they may be doing it harm by encouraging aphids. So the question of whether ants can be used as agents of biological control remains unanswered. However, the ants do not tend all aphids, and those that they do not tend they will eat, thus reducing the numbers of these as well as the caterpillars. Ants may also eat other insects which are problematical to man in ways other than as pests of trees. Thus, larvae of biting flies will be devoured along with everything else and numbers thus reduced.

Ants are generally beneficial to the soil because, rather like earthworms they are able to mix it and improve soil structure.

Ants can usually be regarded as pests when they invade buildings. A number of so-called tramp species, imported into the British Isles from other countries, survive only in buildings which are heated. Ants are basically insects of warm regions and thus heated buildings and greenhouses can form an ideal habitat.

Lasius niger is a common visitor to the larder in summer, especially if the jam-pot lid is not secure or the sugar has not been properly covered. The ant is less a pest here than a nuisance, but it is undoubtedly desirable to eliminate it. The usual practice is to put out a sugary bait laced with a poison, but the trick is to have one that is not immediately fatal. Because of their food-sharing behaviour, trophallaxis, this poison will be passed around the colony, even to brood, even if only a few workers get it. This serves to eliminate the whole nest if the method works well.

A whole range of exotic species has become established in greenhouses, such as those in botanical gardens. These include *Hypoponera punctatissima, Pheidole megacephala* (in which the workers, as the name suggests, have very large heads), *Iridomyrmex humilis, Tapinoma melanocephalum, Paratrechina longicornis* and *P. vividula.*

The best known tramp inhabiting buildings is the Pharaoh's Ant *(Monomorium pharaonis).* This species requires particularly hot conditions and is commonest in buildings which are kept hot throughout the year. It has been a notorious pest in hospitals. It will nest in all kinds of nooks and crannies and can invade almost any suitably hot and humid place. Its feeding habits are equally catholic. Workers of *Monomorium* are very tiny (0.1 inch, 2 to 2.5 mm) and colonies vary in size from a few hundred to a few thousand workers. *Monomorium* has proved very difficult to control because all scraps of food must be eliminated. A promising method, developed in the 1970s, involves baiting the food with an insect hormone called juvenile hormone, which causes disruption of larval moulting and egg laying. It seems to be the best method devised so far for getting rid of this otherwise intractable pest.

Simple identification guide

Because a number of the British species are uncommon and very small, they are unlikely to be encountered by anyone but the specialist. The following short key concentrates, therefore, on those species most likely to be encountered. The key covers workers only. Books listed on page 24 should be consulted if in doubt.

Start at the beginning of the key. Each clue has two alternatives. Decide which applies to the ant being examined. When this has been done, look at the number on the right, and refer to that clue. For example if, in clue 1, you decide that the ant has a two-segmented waist, then you should go to clue 9, and so on. If you find that the ant does not fit either clue at any point, you have probably made a wrong decision somewhere and you should start again from the beginning. When you reach a genus or species name you should read the notes in brackets and see if these fit the specimen, locality, behaviour and so on.

A hand lens may be needed to see some of the features clearly.

1. Ants with one-segmented waist (see figure 1).   2.
    Ants with two-segmented waist (see figure 2).   9.

2. Some workers 7 mm (0.25 inch) or more in
    length.   3.
    All workers smaller than this.   7.

3. Reddish in colour, at least in part.   4.
    Colour other than reddish, generally black.   6.

4. Margin of clypeus notched (see figure 18).   *Formica sanguinea* (southern Britain only, often mixed nests with *F. fusca)*.

    Margin of clypeus not notched.   5.

5. Head deeply notched at back (see figure 14).   *Formica exsecta* (around Bournemouth and in Cairngorms only).
    Head not like this.   *Formica rufa/aquilonia/lugubris* (see figure 18 to separate).

6. Shining black, head notched at back.   *Lasius fuliginosus* (nests usually at base of tree stumps, very shiny ant, forms trails).
    Not like this, dull black.   *Formica fusca/lemani* (difficult to separate, very active large ants, small colonies).

7. Workers yellow, nest a soil mound.   *Lasius flavus* (nests an earthen mound with vegetation on top; nest density often very high, hundreds in a field).

    Workers not yellow.   8.

23

8.	Workers black, hairy body.	*Lasius niger* (if not truly the commonest British species, certainly the most often seen).
	Workers black, body not all hairy.	*Tapinoma erraticum* (workers tiny and very active in sunny weather; they run with gaster raised).
9.	In nests of *Formica rufa*.	*Formicoxenus nitidulus* (would have to be carefully looked for; nests in twigs inside other nest).
	Independent colonies.	10.
10.	Workers black with square shoulders.	*Tetramorium caespitium* (the only dark two-petioled ant likely to be found; southern Britain only).
	Not like this.	11.
11.	Last three antennal segments shorter than rest of funiculus.	*Myrmica* species (eight species very similar; consult specialist work).
	Last three antennal segments about as long as rest of funiculus.	*Leptothorax* species.

Further reading

Bolton, B., and Collingwood, C. A. *Hymenoptera, Formicidae*. Handbooks for the Identification for British Insects, volume VI, part 3(c), 1975.
Brian, M. V. *Ants*. Collins, New Naturalist Series, 1977.
Chauvin, R. *The World of Ants*. Gollancz, 1969.
Harde, K. W. (edited by Hammond, P. W.). *A Field Guide in Colour to Beetles*. Octopus Books, 1984. (For pictures of some myrmecophilous beetles.)

ACKNOWLEDGEMENTS
The author records his gratitude to John Whittaker for introducing him to ants, to Pete Flint for his continued help, and to his wife, Ann, for assisting him throughout this and many other projects. Illustrations are acknowledged to: Sean Burgess, 2, 3, 18; Robin Fletcher (Natural Image), 12; Jeremy Thomas (Biofotos), 23; Peter Wilson (Natural Image), 6. All other illustrations are by the author.